IMPACT ACADEMY

fueling growth, inspiring action

A nonprofit's guide to
social media marketing

By Alec Avedissian

This guide is structured to walk you through each aspect of social media marketing step by step:

I. Introduction

II. Understanding the Algorithm

III. How to Select Viral Clips

IV. Defining Your Nonprofit's Niche

V. Niche Research

VI. Branding

VII. Fundraising Blueprint

VIII. Best Practices for Enhancing Supporter Engagement

IX. Convert Viewers to Supporters

X. Conclusion and Best Practices

I. Introduction

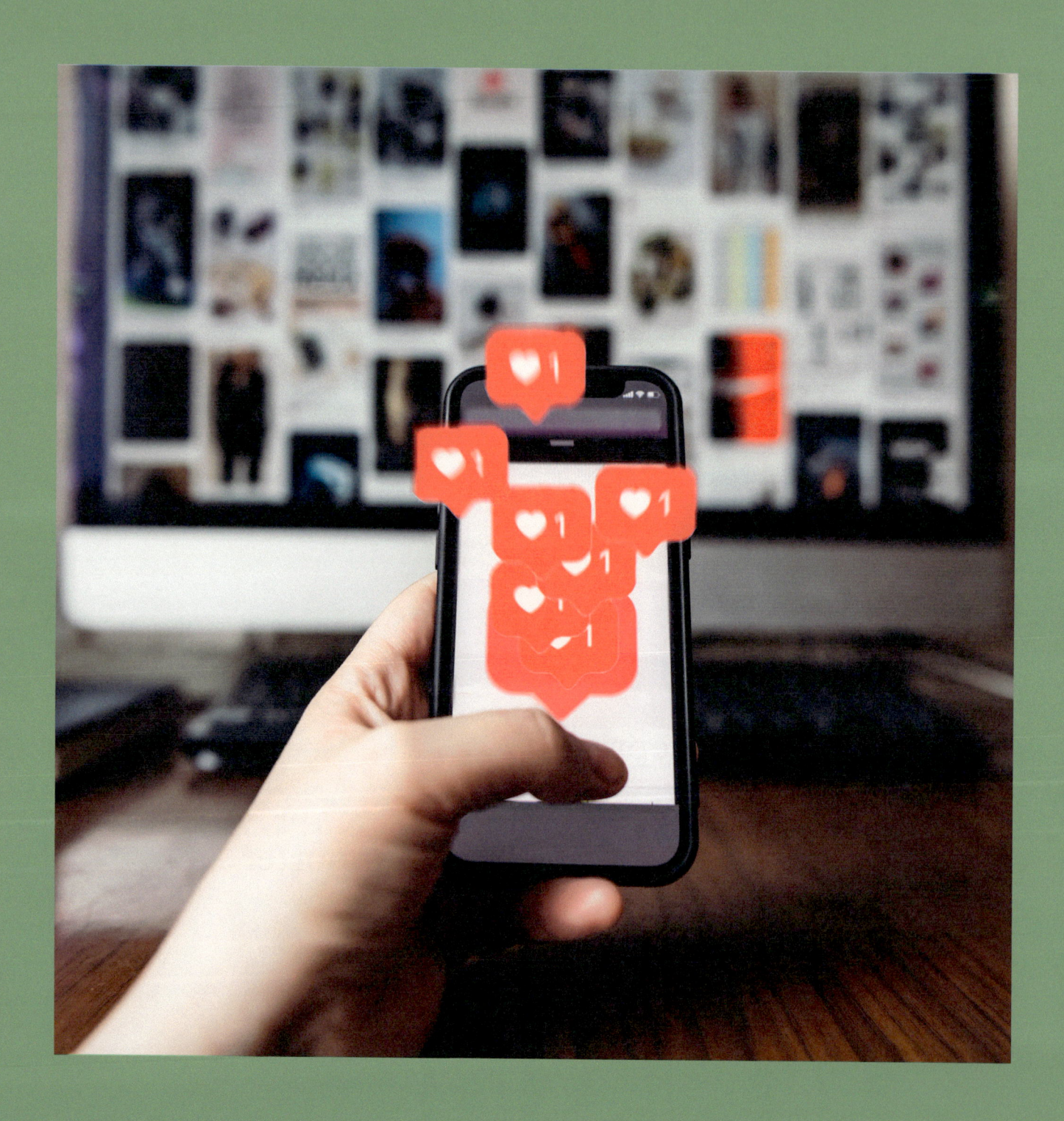

Welcome to "Impact Academy: Fueling Growth, Inspiring Action", a comprehensive guide designed specifically for nonprofits looking to leverage the power of social media marketing to amplify their message, engage their audience, and scale their impact. In a digital era where attention is the currency, understanding and navigating the intricacies of social media platforms can be the difference between being heard and being overlooked.

At Impact Academy, we believe in nonprofits' transformative power and ability to drive positive change. However, even the most passionate and purpose-driven organizations struggle to reach their audience in the crowded digital landscape. This is where we step in. Our guide is not just a collection of strategies and tips; it's a roadmap on how to make your cause resonate with people around the world.

From deciphering the algorithms that dictate what content gets attention to optimizing your social media presence for maximum engagement, this workbook is designed to be your companion in the journey toward making a more significant impact. We cover everything from the basics of understanding social media algorithms, which are crucial for gaining visibility and engagement, to selecting content that has the potential to go viral, ensuring your message spreads far and wide.

Our goal is to equip you with the knowledge and tools you need to navigate the social media landscape confidently and make your mark on the world. Your mission is our passion, and together, we can maximize positive impact.

II. Algorithm Optimization Guide: Amplifying Your Voice

Understanding and fine-tuning your approach to social media algorithms is paramount in ensuring your message reaches the widest possible audience. Each social media platform, be it TikTok, Instagram, or Facebook, operates on its unique algorithm, but the foundational elements of optimization are universally applicable.

Common Algorithm Factors:

♥ 142 💬 37 👤 27

1. Watch Time:

The cumulative duration for which users engage with your video content.

Importance:
Platforms prioritize content that captivates users for extended periods.

Example:
Consider the World Wildlife Fund's (WWF) engaging storytelling through video content that highlights their conservation efforts, keeping viewers hooked and thereby promoting their content further.

2. Engagement:

The sum of interactions your content receives, including likes, comments, and shares.

Importance:

A high level of engagement signals to the platform that your content is resonating with users.

Example:

The ALS Association's Ice Bucket Challenge became a viral sensation, demonstrating how compelling calls to action can significantly boost user interaction and visibility.

3. Retention Rate:

The proportion of viewers that stay engaged with a video until the end.

Importance:
Content that retains viewers' attention until the last second is often deemed high-quality by algorithms and thus promoted more.

Example:
Charity: Water's captivating storytelling in their campaign videos often results in high retention rates, as viewers are drawn into the narrative and watch through to the end.

Your Nonprofit's Content Creation Checklist:

1. Compelling Start:
Begin videos with a strong hook to grab attention immediately

2. Emotional Storytelling:
Use storytelling that connects emotionally, making viewers invested in your narrative.

3. Interactive Elements:
Incorporate polls, questions, or direct calls for viewer input to make content interactive.

4. Value-Added Content:
Provide content that offers educational insights, actionable advice, or unique perspectives on your cause.

Your Nonprofit's Content Creation Checklist:

5. Dynamic Pacing:
Maintain a balance between fast-paced segments and reflective moments to keep viewers engaged.

6. Visual and Auditory Quality:
Ensure high-quality visuals and clear audio to enhance the viewing experience.

7. Community Engagement:
Encourage viewers to share their stories or participate in challenges related to your cause.

8. Clear Call-to-Action:
Conclude with a compelling call-to-action, guiding viewers on what to do next.

III. Selecting Viral Clips: A Guide for Maximum Engagement

Crafting short, impactful clips from your longer content is an art, especially when trying to captivate audiences on fast-paced platforms like Instagram and TikTok. Here's how to do it effectively, with insights drawn from successful nonprofit campaigns:

1. *Strategic Content Selection:*
Identify moments that resonate deeply or reveal unexpected insights. For instance, Habitat for Humanity frequently shares transformative stories, showcasing the life-changing impact of safe, affordable housing on families and communities, emphasizing the profound difference a home can make.

2. Powerful Openings:

Craft an opening that captivates instantly. Greenpeace effectively uses striking visuals of environmental beauty or degradation to immediately draw viewers into their message of conservation and activism.

3. Authentic Moments:
Genuine, unscripted moments enhance the connection with your audience. The Trevor Project shares heartfelt testimonials from LGBTQ+ youth, offering a sincere look into the lives of those they support, which can profoundly resonate with viewers.

THE TREVOR PROJECT
Saving Young LGBTQ Lives

4. Focus on Replay Value:

Aim for content that invites repeated viewing. Ocean Conservancy shares captivating underwater footage, highlighting the mesmerizing beauty of marine life and the importance of preserving our oceans, encouraging viewers to return and watch again.

5. Learning from the Best: Take cues from top content creators across various platforms. Feeding America leverages the power of storytelling and influencer collaborations to bring attention to the issue of hunger in America, adopting a style that resonates with a wide audience.

6. Interactive Dynamics:
Look for content with lively and engaging interactions. The ACLU often features debates, speeches, and interviews that highlight critical civil liberties issues, engaging viewers with the dynamic exchange of ideas and perspectives.

ACLU
AMERICAN CIVIL LIBERTIES UNION

Activity: Crafting Clips with Viral Potential

Elevating your nonprofit's message through viral clips requires a keen eye for compelling content and a strategic approach to editing and sharing. As you refine your process, keep these key points in mind for creating content that resonates and spreads widely.

Your Nonprofit's Viral Clip Checklist:

- [ ] Does your clip have a moment that tugs at heartstrings or raises eyebrows?
- [ ] Does your clip start with a hook that immediately grabs attention?
- [ ] Is there a raw, authentic moment that enhances relatability?
- [ ] Will viewers want to watch this clip more than once?
- [ ] Have you incorporated successful elements observed in popular content creators' work?
- [ ] Does your clip feature engaging exchanges or reactions?
- [ ] Does the clip clearly reflect and promote your nonprofit's mission and values?
- [ ] Does the clip end with a clear, compelling call to action, encouraging viewers to engage further with your cause?

IV. Defining Your Nonprofit's Niche

Identifying and embracing your nonprofit's niche is crucial for crafting impactful short-form content that resonates with your target audience. This tailored approach ensures your message not only reaches the right ears but also prompts action and support. Here's how to refine your focus and leverage your unique position in the nonprofit sector:

1. Market Awareness:

Recognize the competitive nature of the digital landscape for nonprofits. Keep up with emerging trends, popular themes in content, and innovative engagement strategies employed by similar organizations. Understanding what others are doing can inspire your strategies and help you stand out.

2. Learn from Leaders:

Look to leading nonprofits within your sphere for inspiration. Analyze how they communicate their mission, engage their audience, and drive action. This could involve storytelling techniques, engagement strategies, or ways they highlight their impact.

3. Content Strategy Blueprint:

Develop a clear and concise content creation plan that aligns with your mission and resonates with your audience. Whether it's through educational pieces, success stories, or behind-the-scenes glimpses, ensure each piece of content clearly ties back to your core message.

4. Embrace Current Trends:

Stay attuned to the latest trends within the nonprofit sector and broader social issues that align with your mission. Utilizing trending topics can increase the relevance and reach of your content, making your message more likely to be shared and discussed.

5. Algorithm-Savvy Content:

Craft content with social media algorithms in mind, focusing on elements that drive engagement such as compelling narratives, strong calls to action, and interactive features. This strategic approach can help amplify your content's visibility.

6. Professional Presentation:

While thumbnails might hold varying degrees of importance across platforms, maintaining a consistent and professional visual identity can enhance your nonprofit's credibility and attract a more engaged following.

Aligning Passion with Purpose

Your niche is not just a sector you work within; it's a reflection of your passion and purpose. By aligning your content with what genuinely inspires your team and resonates with your audience, you'll foster deeper connections and drive meaningful action. Remember, the most successful nonprofits are those that stay true to their mission while adeptly navigating the digital landscape to amplify their message.

Activity

- Does your content clearly reflect your nonprofit's mission and values?

- Have you analyzed successful nonprofits for strategies that could be adapted to your context?

- Are you incorporating relevant trends to make your content more engaging and shareable?

- Is there a clear plan linking each piece of content back to your core message?

- Does your content cater to the algorithms by encouraging viewer interaction and engagement?

- Are your visuals, including thumbnails when applicable, consistent and reflective of your nonprofit's brand and professionalism?

V. Niche Research

Understanding your nonprofit's niche in depth is crucial for carving out a distinctive space in a crowded field. This involves not just identifying the unique aspects of your mission and audience but also staying abreast of trends, strategies, and the evolving digital ecosystem. Here's how to conduct effective niche research to enhance your nonprofit's outreach and impact:

1. Discover Your Niche:

Start by defining the unique space your nonprofit occupies, considering your mission, the communities you serve, and the change you aim to create. Reflect on what sets your organization apart and how this distinctiveness can be communicated through compelling content.

2. Algorithm Adaptation:

Tailor your content strategy to the preferences of social media algorithms. For example, engaging with content similar to your own can signal platforms like Instagram or Facebook about your niche, potentially increasing the visibility of your posts among like-minded audiences.

3. Community Engagement:

Build relationships within your niche by interacting with other nonprofits and related accounts. Commenting, sharing, and collaborating can foster a sense of community and enhance your visibility through algorithmic associations.

4. Research Repository:

Create a centralized database (using tools like Google Docs or a digital notebook) to collect inspiring content, innovative fundraising campaigns, or compelling storytelling examples. This resource can become an invaluable reference for brainstorming and strategy development.

5. Focused Analysis:

Avoid passive consumption of content; instead, actively analyze what makes certain posts successful. Note the storytelling techniques, visual styles, and engagement prompts that seem to resonate most within your niche.

6. Creative Evolution:

Allow your content and editing style to evolve based on your research findings. Revisit your saved content periodically to refresh your creative approach and ensure your messaging remains relevant and engaging.

Activity:
Niche Research Checklist for Nonprofits

Regularly test different content formats, storytelling techniques, and calls-to-action to see what resonates best with your audience. Successful elements from high-performing posts can be adapted and iterated upon to refine your content strategy continually.

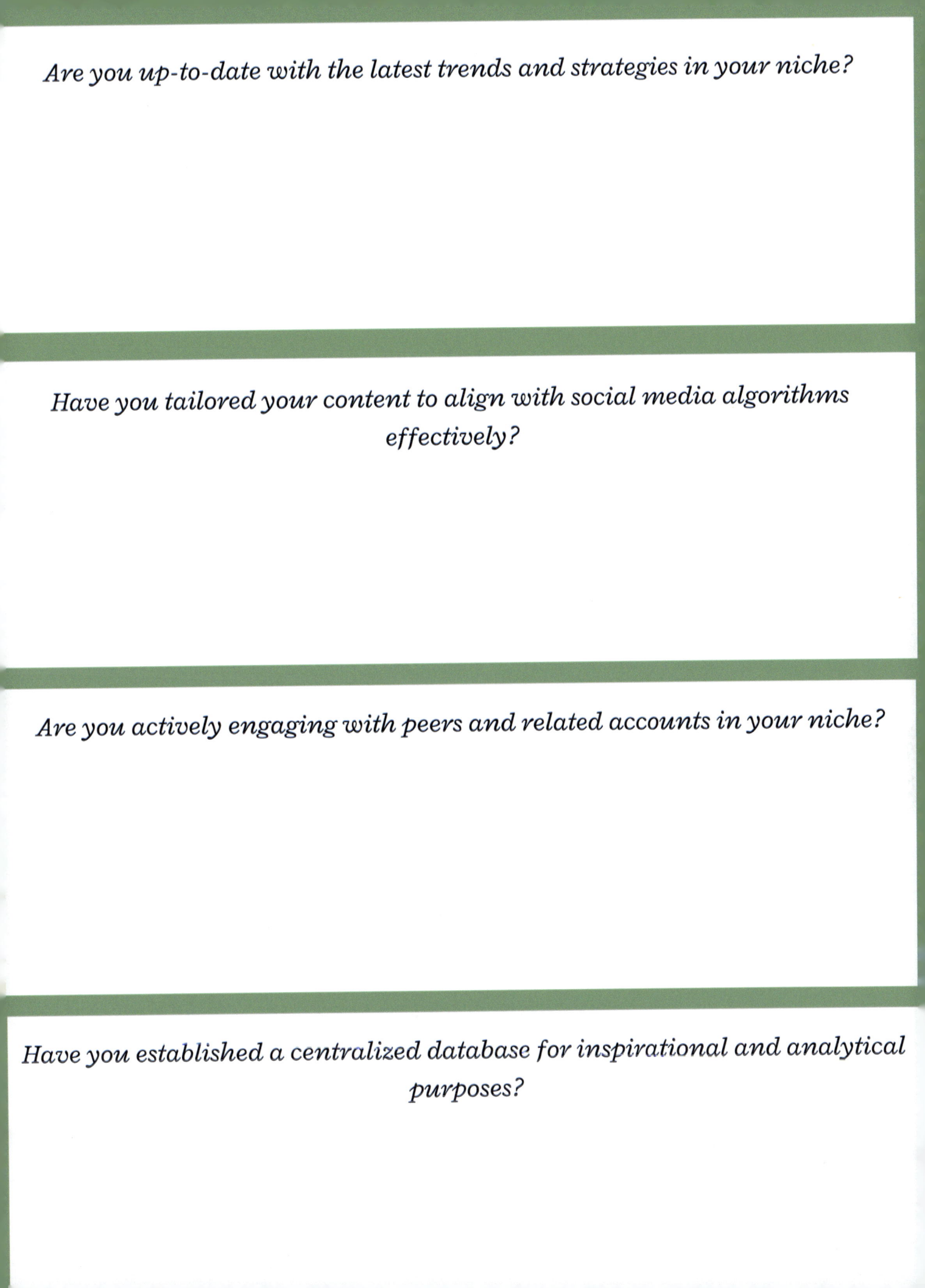

Are you up-to-date with the latest trends and strategies in your niche?

Have you tailored your content to align with social media algorithms effectively?

Are you actively engaging with peers and related accounts in your niche?

Have you established a centralized database for inspirational and analytical purposes?

Do you actively analyze successful content to understand why it works?

Are you allowing your content strategy to evolve based on insights gained from your research?

Are you experimenting with your content to identify what achieves the best engagement and impact?

V. Branding

Branding is more than just a logo or color scheme; it's the embodiment of your nonprofit's mission, values, and the impact you aim to create. A strong brand identity resonates with your audience, builds trust, and enhances your visibility in your niche. Here's how to refine your branding to make a lasting impression:

1. Distinctive Brand Identity:

Begin by crafting a brand identity that stands out. This includes a cohesive visual style for your content, from the color palette to the font choices, ensuring your nonprofit is instantly recognizable to your audience. This consistency in branding helps forge a stronger connection with your viewers.

2. Brand Marking:

Similar to watermarking, incorporate your nonprofit's logo, name, or acronyms subtly into your content. This not only safeguards your material but also serves as a constant reminder of your brand, enhancing brand recall among your audience.

3. Consistent Quality

Align your branding efforts with the consistent delivery of high-quality content. Ensure that every piece of content, whether a video, image, or post, reflects the standards and ethos of your nonprofit, reinforcing a positive brand image.

4. Memorable Visual Identity:

Carefully design your profile picture and choose a username that's both reflective of your nonprofit's identity and easy to remember. This visual identity acts as a digital 'first impression' and plays a crucial role in attracting and retaining followers.

5. Strategic Launch:

Hold off on launching your social media page or campaign until you've established a cohesive and polished branding strategy. A well-presented brand makes a stronger impact and can significantly boost engagement right from the start.

6. Leveraging Editing Tools:

Utilize editing tools and presets to maintain a consistent style and quality in your content. This can include branded graphics, themed filters, or animated elements that align with your brand's personality, making content creation more efficient and cohesive.

A well-defined brand identity not only distinguishes your nonprofit in a crowded space but also cultivates a sense of trust and loyalty among your audience. By implementing these branding strategies, your organization can enhance its visibility, foster deeper connections with your audience, and ultimately drive more significant impact.

Activity

| Is your content's visual style consistently aligned with your brand identity? | Are you subtly incorporating your brand logo or initials in your content to enhance brand recall? | Does every piece of content reflect the high standards and values of your nonprofit? |

Activity

Are your profile picture and username clear, memorable, and reflective of your brand?

Have you developed a cohesive branding strategy before launching your campaign or social media page?

Are you utilizing editing tools and presets to maintain consistent branding across your content?

VII. Fundraising Blueprint

Leveraging short-form content for fundraising involves strategically guiding viewers from initial engagement to active support. This process, often visualized as a funnel, is crucial for nonprofits aiming to transform viral moments into meaningful contributions. Here's how to craft an effective fundraising funnel using short-form content:

1. Engagement Hook:

Start with content that instantly grabs attention. This could be an impactful statistic, a compelling story, or a captivating visual related to your cause. The goal is to make viewers pause and take notice.

2. Emotional Connection:

Use the power of storytelling to forge an emotional connection with your audience. Share real stories of those impacted by your work or demonstrate the tangible results of your efforts. Emotional engagement is key to moving viewers down the funnel.

3. Mission Alignment:

Ensure that each piece of content clearly reflects your mission and the change you aim to create. This alignment helps viewers understand the importance of your work and why their support matters.

4. Clear Call-to-Action (CTA):

Every piece of content should include a clear, compelling CTA that guides viewers on how they can support your cause. Whether it's donating, signing a petition, or sharing the content with their network, make the action step obvious and straightforward.

5. Seamless Donation Process:

Optimize the donation process to be as seamless as possible. Use direct links to your donation page and ensure the page is mobile-friendly and easy to navigate. The fewer barriers to donation, the better.

6. Impact Transparency:

Share content that highlights the impact of donations. Showcasing success stories and updates builds trust and encourages ongoing support by showing viewers the real difference their contributions make.

The effectiveness of your fundraising funnel hinges on the quality of your content and the strategic design of the funnel itself. By captivating viewers with engaging content, forging an emotional connection, and guiding them through a clear and easy process to support your cause, you can convert short-form content success into tangible fundraising achievements.

Activity

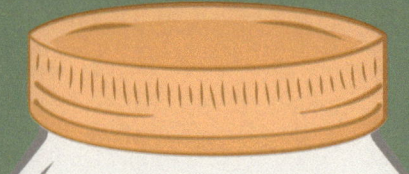

- Does your content immediately grab viewers' attention and highlight your cause?

- Are you effectively using stories to connect emotionally with your audience?

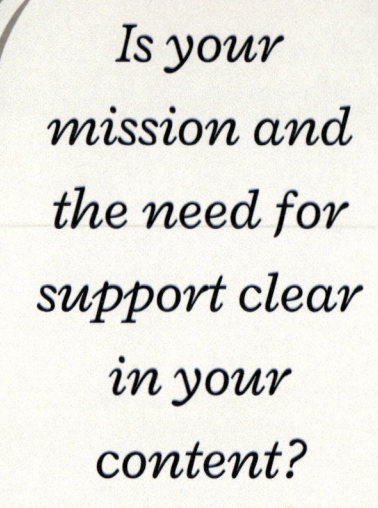

- Is your mission and the need for support clear in your content?

- Are your calls-to-action clear, compelling, and easy to follow?

- Is the donation process straightforward and accessible from mobile devices?

- Are you transparently showing the impact of donations to build trust and encourage further support?

VIII. Best Practices for Enhancing Supporter Engagement

Engaging supporters is pivotal for nonprofits to sustain and expand their impact. By nurturing a strong connection with your audience, you foster a community that's actively involved and invested in your cause. Here are some best practices to elevate supporter engagement:

1. Personalized Communication

Tailor your communication to address your supporters by name and recognize their previous contributions. Personalization makes supporters feel valued and more connected to your cause.

2. Interactive Content:

Incorporate interactive elements like polls, quizzes, and Q&A sessions in your content strategy. These tools not only increase engagement but also provide valuable insights into your supporters' preferences and opinions.

3. Regular Updates:

Keep your supporters in the loop with regular updates about your projects, achievements, and the tangible impact of their contributions. Transparency fosters trust and strengthens supporter relationships.

4. Acknowledgment and Appreciation:

Regularly acknowledge and express gratitude for your supporters' contributions. Recognition can be public, through social media shoutouts, or private, via personalized thank-you messages.

5. Community Building:

Create spaces for your supporters to interact, share stories, and be part of a larger community. This could be through online forums, social media groups, or virtual events.

6. Engagement Analytics:

Monitor engagement metrics to understand what content resonates with your supporters. Use these insights to refine your engagement strategies and content offerings.

7. Responsive Feedback Loops:

Encourage and act on feedback from your supporters. Showing that you value their opinions and are willing to make changes based on their feedback enhances engagement and loyalty.

8. Involvement Opportunities:

Provide various ways for supporters to get involved beyond financial contributions. This could include volunteering, advocacy, or participating in awareness campaigns.

The strength of your relationship with your supporters directly influences the effectiveness of your engagement strategies. By implementing these best practices, you can create a vibrant community of supporters who are actively engaged and committed to your cause.

Activity

> Are you personalizing your interactions with supporters to make them feel valued?

> Do you regularly include interactive content to engage your audience?

> Are you consistently sharing updates and achievements with your supporters?

> Do you have a system in place to regularly thank and recognize your supporters?

Activity

> Have you established platforms or forums for your supporters to connect and engage?

> Are you offering varied opportunities for supporters to engage with your cause beyond donations?

> Are you tracking engagement metrics to guide your content and communication strategies?

> Do you actively solicit and respond to feedback from your supporters?

IX. Convert Viewers to Supporters

For nonprofits, converting viewers into supporters is crucial for driving mission impact. Strategic Calls to Action (CTAs) in your short-form content can guide viewers towards meaningful engagement with your cause. Here's how to craft CTAs that resonate and motivate action:

1. CTAs in Visuals:
 - Design your video thumbnails with text overlays that encourage viewers to learn more or take action. This visual prompt should be clear and compelling, guiding viewers to your next desired step.
 - Example: "Join Us in Making a Change - Details in Bio!"

2. CTAs in Audio:
 - Integrate a memorable and inspiring message within your video's audio track. This auditory CTA can echo your mission and invite viewers to engage further with your cause.
 - Example: "Be the change you wish to see! Learn more in our bio."

3. CTAs in Descriptions:
 - Utilize the video description or captions to embed a direct CTA. This text should be concise and action-oriented, guiding viewers on how they can contribute or participate.
 - Example: "Help us reach our goal by donating through the link in our bio."

4. Engaging through Comments:
 - Actively engage with comments on your posts. Use these interactions as opportunities to share more information or direct interested viewers to your website or donation page.
 - Example: "Reply 'Impact' for more info on how you can help!"

Diverse and creative CTAs across your content can significantly boost viewer-to-supporter conversion rates. By incorporating clear and compelling action steps in your visuals, audio, descriptions, and comment interactions, you make it easy for viewers to take the next step in supporting your cause. Remember, the effectiveness of your CTAs lies in their clarity, relevance, and the ease with which viewers can respond.

Are your video thumbnails designed with clear, action-invoking text?

Are your video descriptions and captions equipped with direct CTAs?

Are you using comment interactions to further engage viewers and guide them towards supporting your cause?

Does your video's audio include a memorable call to action?

ACTIVITY

X. Conclusion and Best Practices

As we wrap up Impact Academy, it's clear that leveraging social media effectively is key to amplifying your nonprofit's message and engaging with a broader audience. By understanding algorithms, crafting compelling content, and strategically employing calls to action, your organization can significantly enhance its online presence and impact. Here are the best practices to keep in mind as you navigate the dynamic world of social media:

1. *Stay Authentic:*
Always ensure your content aligns with your mission and values. Authenticity resonates with audiences and builds trust in your nonprofit.

2. *Engage Consistently:*
Regular interaction with your followers, through comments, messages, and community posts, fosters a sense of community and loyalty.

3. *Use Data Wisely:*
Analyze performance metrics to understand what content works best for your audience. Use these insights to refine your strategy and content.

4. *Be Adaptable:*
Social media trends and algorithms change frequently. Stay flexible and be willing to adjust your strategies to maintain engagement and visibility.

5. Leverage Multimedia
Utilize a mix of video, images, and text to keep your content diverse and engaging. Different formats can highlight various aspects of your work.

6. Highlight Impact:
Regularly share stories and updates about the real-world impact of your work. Showing tangible results encourages support and advocacy.

7. Collaborate and Network:
Partner with other nonprofits, influencers, and brands to expand your reach. Collaborations can introduce your cause to new audiences.